HAUNTED HOUSES

Alex Summers

Guided Reading Level: **T**

ROurke
Educational Media

rourkeeducationalmedia.com

Scan for Related Titles
and Teacher Resources

TABLE OF CONTENTS

STRANGE SENSATIONS

Do you ever feel like someone is watching you, but there's no one there? No one you can see, anyway.

Cold spots, unexplained noises, and the sense you're not alone in a house can make you think, "Yikes! It's haunted!"

Hauntings are reported at homes all over the world—Including the U.S. president's home.

Paranormal, or supernatural, activity is not explained by science or the laws of nature. A haunting is considered a supernatural occurrence.

HAUNTED WHITE HOUSE

The White House is haunted? **Rumor** is 1600 Pennsylvania Avenue in Washington, D.C., the most famous U.S. address, is teeming with paranormal activity.

The most frequently reported sighting in the White House is the ghost, or spirit, of the 16th president, Abraham Lincoln.

ASSASSINATION OF PRESIDENT LINCOLN, FORD'S THEATRE, WASHINGTON, APRIL 14, 1865.

His wife, Mary, held many **séances** in the White House, which the president attended. Lincoln was said to have predicted his own death more than once before it happened.

President Lincoln's life was cut **tragically** short by an **assassin's** bullet in April 1865. His spirit may remain as a result of his traumatic demise.

Other presidents, such as Harry Truman and Andrew Jackson, make ghostly appearances to White House visitors, as well.

AMITYVILLE HORROR HOUSE

112 Ocean Avenue, in Amityville, N.Y. is not a place you want to visit alone, or maybe at all!

Ronald DeFeo Jr. testified that he heard voices, which told him to murder his family.

In 1974, six members of the DeFeo family were killed in that house by their oldest son. The following year it was sold, but it did not come unoccupied.

Police divers search the family swimming pool for the .35 caliber Marlin rifle allegedly used by Ronald (Butch) DeFeo to murder his father, mother, and four younger siblings.

The new owners, George and Kathy Lutz, reported a tormented ghost who ripped doors from hinges and slammed cabinets. They also reported seeing demonic faces and swarms of insects inside the house. Yikes!

They recounted their story to a writer named Jay Anson, who published *The Amityville Horror: A True Story*, in 1977.

The book became a best-seller, followed by a film that sparked nearly a half-dozen sequels. This horrifying story spooked millions of people. But is it true?

Actor Ryan Reynolds played George Lutz in the 2005 movie based on the horrifying experiences the family endured after purchasing what they thought would be their "dream home."

VILLISCA AX MURDER HOUSE

On Thursday, June 13, 1912, two adults and six children were found **brutally** murdered in their beds in the small mid-western town of Villisca, Iowa.

The murders were never solved, and a sense of gloom still **lingers** in the home. Many believe that the spirits of the murdered family still remain here, their ghosts haunting the old house where they tragically died.

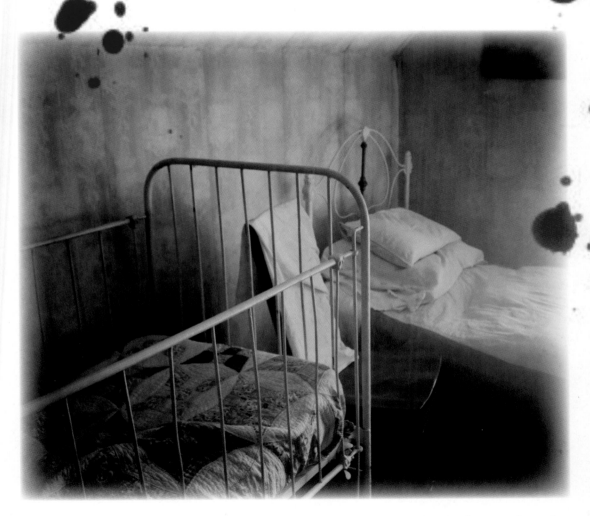

We will never know what happened that dark night inside the home of J.B. and Sarah Moore. Given the many years that have passed, the killer's dark secret was carried to their own grave.

Tours of the home have been cut short by falling lamps, moving objects, and banging sounds. Some psychics have claimed to communicate with the spirits of the dead there.

A pan of bloody water was discovered on the kitchen table as well as a plate of uneaten food.

It is believed that sometime between midnight and 5 a.m., an unknown assailant entered the home of J.B. Moore and brutally murdered all occupants of the house.

Paranormal investigators and thrill-seekers who have stayed overnight claim they were awoken by the sounds of children's voices. Others have captured mysterious audio, video, and photographic evidence suggesting something supernatural lurks within the walls.

BORGVATTNET
(THE HAUNTED VICARAGE)

Moving objects, screams, shadow people, and an old rocking chair that keeps rocking?

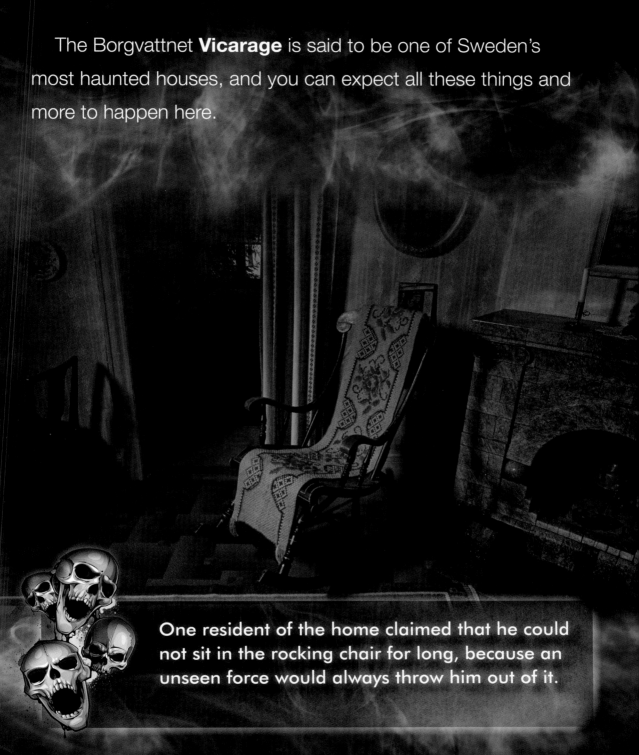

The Borgvattnet **Vicarage** is said to be one of Sweden's most haunted houses, and you can expect all these things and more to happen here.

One resident of the home claimed that he could not sit in the rocking chair for long, because an unseen force would always throw him out of it.

In the early 1980s, a priest named Tore Forslund attempted to perform an exorcism on the house. It was unsuccessful.

The first documented account of paranormal activity at the vicarage happened in 1927, when a resident chaplain reported that he witnessed his laundry being torn down from the line by an unseen force in the attic.

The vicarage is now a bed and breakfast for those curious enough to stay the night. Anyone who makes it through the night receives a diploma to mark their bravery.

One guest was awakened in the middle of the night with a feeling she was being watched. She saw three old women sitting on a sofa against one wall in the room. They all appeared to be crying.

THE MOLLY BROWN HOUSE

The Molly Brown House is in Denver, Colorado. Molly died in 1932 and soon after ... well, let's just say Molly never really left. At least not her ghostly form.

MOLLY BROWN
HOUSE MUSEUM
A PROPERTY OF HISTORIC DENVER INC.

Public tours are held at the Molly Brown House. If you're lucky, you may spot some apparitions, or hear some phantom piano music.

An apparition of a woman in a long dress is often seen sitting at the dining room table. She is also known to rearrange the chairs.

Visitors sometimes report smelling pipe smoke in the attic and the basement. This is where J.J. Brown, Molly's husband, might have snuck down to smoke his pipe—away from his disapproving wife.

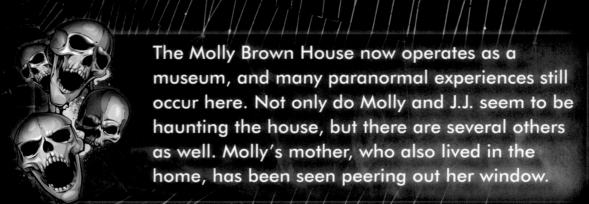

The Molly Brown House now operates as a museum, and many paranormal experiences still occur here. Not only do Molly and J.J. seem to be haunting the house, but there are several others as well. Molly's mother, who also lived in the home, has been seen peering out her window.

WHAT CAUSES A HAUNTING?

Many haunted houses are very old with a lot of history. Births, deaths, traumatic events, and strong emotions have occurred in these homes.

But what turns an ordinary, everyday house into something spooky?

Believers in the paranormal think hauntings happen for different reasons. Sometimes when a spirit appears it is to say goodbye to a loved one. Other times, a ghost may have more sinister intentions.

An earthbound spirit may have died so quickly that they are unaware of being dead.

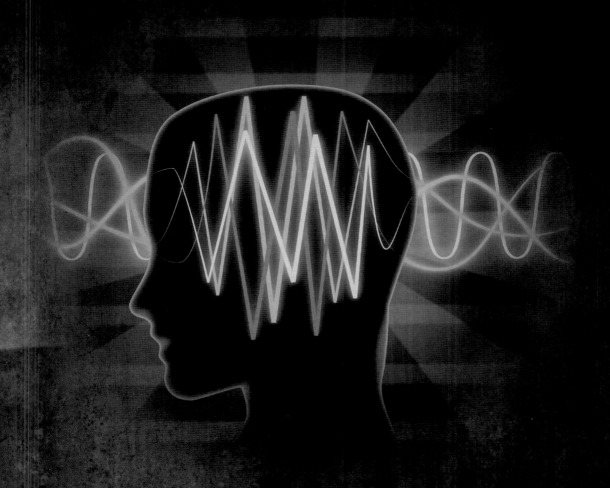

Spirits are thought to remain as trapped energy. In this condition, they may attach to a living person's energy field.

One theory about hauntings is that they are imprints left in the Earth's energy field. Some scientists accept that brain waves emit an electrical field that can affect and enhance spirit activity.

Some people think the **residual** energy from a deceased person may linger in a home, especially if they died there with unfinished business. This may compel the person's spirit to continue to reach out to the living.

Or if something terrible happened in a home, dark or evil spirits may be drawn there by the negative energy created by that event.

What do you believe?

HAUNTED HOUSES WORLD MAP

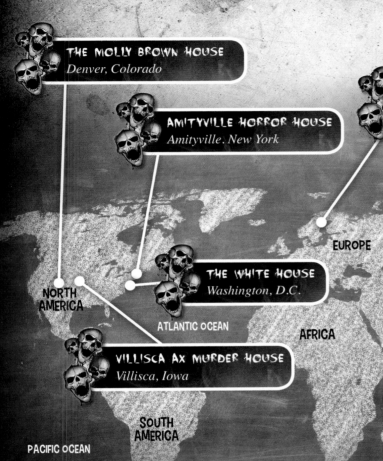

THE MOLLY BROWN HOUSE
Denver, Colorado

AMITYVILLE HORROR HOUSE
Amityville, New York

BORGVATTNET VICARAGE
Borgvattnet, Sweden

ARCTIC SEA

EUROPE

THE WHITE HOUSE
Washington, D.C.

ASIA

NORTH
AMERICA

ATLANTIC OCEAN

AFRICA

VILLISCA AX MURDER HOUSE
Villisca, Iowa

SOUTH
AMERICA

AUSTRALIA

PACIFIC OCEAN

SOUTHERN OCEAN

GLOSSARY

assassins (uh-SAS-uhnz): people hired to murder someone who is well-known or famous

brutally (BRUH-tuhl-ee): to do something in an extremely cruel or violent way

lingers (LING-uhrz): being slow in leaving or continuing to stay

residual (RUH-zi-dyoo-uhl): the remains of something left over

rumor (ROO-mur): a story that is spread by mouth but may not be true

séances (SAY-ahn-siz): meetings where people try to contact the dead

tragically (TRAJ-ik-lee): when someone has died or suffered in a shocking or cruel way

vicarage (vik-uhr-ij): the residence or home of a vicar, or holy man such as a priest